So well I know these woods I half believe

There is an intimate fellowship we share;

So many years we breathed the same brave air,

Kept spring in common, and were one to grieve

Summer's undoing, saw the fall bereave

Us both of beauty, together learned to bear

The weight of winter:—when I go otherwhere—

An unreturning journey—I would leave

Some whisper of a song in these old oaks,

A footfall lingering till some distant summer

Another singer down these paths may stray—

The destined one a golden future cloaks—

And he may love them, too, this graced newcomer,

And may remember that I passed this way.

Rev. Charles L. O'Donnell, C.S.C.

FOOTFALLS IN TIME
Notre Dame

A PICTORIAL

PHOTOGRAPHED BY
WILLIAM STRODE

1842

HARMONY HOUSE
PUBLISHERS

Acknowledgments

The photographs chosen to document the University's past were selected from the collections of the Notre Dame Archives. Many of these images were made by anonymous photographers whose work was preserved in student scrapbooks. Others were produced by the University Photographer, a position held by M. Bruce Harlan from 1949 until 1993 and by Kevin M. Burke from 1993 until the present. The photographs that were selected represent the great diversity of activities, eras, and people that make up the history of Notre Dame.

The staff of the Notre Dame Archives, in particular Assistant Director Charles Lamb and Marlene Wasikowski, chose these historical images. The captions that identify these photographs were researched by the Archives staff and are as accurate as possible given the anonymity of many of the photographers and their subjects.

Photographers Kevin M. Burke, L. K. Dunn and Heather K. Gollatz of the University's Photography Office and Shannon Renter supplemented William Strode's images of contemporary Notre Dame. As was the case with archival photographs, there is an occasional image from the present whose provenance was not clear and to whose anonymous creator we owe thanks.

Others who contributed substantially to the project were Karen K. Anthony, Ronald A. Brostrom, Richard W. Conklin, Dorothy Corson, Charles F. Lennon, Jr., and Dennis K. Moore.

Published by Harmony House Publishers - Louisville
P.O. Box 90 Prospect, Kentucky 40059
502-228-2010

©2000 Harmony House Publishers
All Rights Reserved.
Second Edition printed in Canada 2001

Archival Photography - Notre Dame Archives
Color Photography © by William Strode

Layout and Design - Boz Johnson
Executive Editor - William Strode

Library of Congress 99-75586
Hardcover International Standard Book Number 1-56469-069-5
Softcover International Standard Book Number 1-56469-081-4

E Sorin c s c

*I*t is possible if the snow is right to stand where a 28–year–old French priest stood on a November day in 1842 and see what he saw when he founded L'Universite de Notre Dame Du Lac– woods and frozen water blanketed in white. Father Edward Sorin had $310 in cash, three log buildings in various stages of disrepair in the wilderness of what would become northern Indiana...and a vision of establishing a great Catholic university.

At this first footfall in time, Notre Dame was a name in anticipation of a university. While a classical collegiate curriculum was established early on, so too were elementary and preparatory programs, was well as a manual labor school. In fact, for several decades the collegiate program never attracted more than a dozen students in any year.

If Notre Dame in its infancy was the child of Sorin's vision and will, its subsequent growth and development were the products of large and powerful social and historical forces. Just as the University was established, the first waves of European immigrants, overwhelmingly Catholic, were reaching America's shores, and Notre Dame's location was within easy reach of cities in which they settled, such as Chicago, Detroit and St. Louis. At the outset Notre Dame's destiny was linked with the

American Catholic immigrant experience, and, indeed, the history of the University was to come to mirror the life of the Catholic Church in the United States.

As Notre Dame entered the 20th Century, it was faced with a choice of a safe future as a Catholic preparatory institution or a risky–for a small Midwestern school with no endowment– decision to compete with firmly established public and private institutions of higher learning, schools with undergraduate, graduate and professional schools and equipped with laboratories, libraries and research facilities.

In the two decades following the First World War, Notre Dame effectively chose the latter course, scrapping the elementary, preparatory and manual labor programs while enlarging its collegiate program and starting fund–raising for physical expansion as well as an endowment. The University became a symbol of the educational striving of ethnic Americans to earn a place in the mainstream of America. And something else happened at this time, something that was to make Notre Dame a national institution–a game called football captured the country's imagination. In an era when anti–Catholicism still was an acceptable prejudice in large segments of American society, the ability of the Fighting

Irish to "win over all" became a symbol of the largely Catholic underclass and its quest for acceptance and success.

Just as the years following World War I saw Notre Dame's reputation enhanced as an undergraduate institution, the years following World War II saw it grow gradually into a more mature university. Entrance requirements and faculty hiring became more selective. The physical plant was expanded into a learning environment that kept in touch with the technology curve. Fund–raising on a level with the nation's best highly selective private universities fueled academic progress across the board. A "small but superb" strategy was put in place for graduate education, while the Law School built upon its reputation as the first Catholic home for legal studies in the United States and an M.B.A. program was launched in 1967. Research became an integral part of the academic mission. Notre Dame's founding religious community, the Congregation of Holy Cross, turned governance over to a predominantly lay Board of Trustees in 1967, and the University admitted women to baccalaureate studies in 1972. Through all of this, Notre Dame was true to its Catholic character, remaining a school where belief sat beside learning and values had equal place with facts.

Over the years, Notre Dame has been a work of many hands. As Frank O'Malley put it so succinctly, "Their blood is in the bricks." From the brothers who accompanied Father Sorin to the sisters who served the needs of 19th Century Notre Dame, from the bachelor dons and their lay successors as professors and administrators to the young men who came to Notre Dame aspiring to a priestly vocation and lived out a ministry here–the mosaic that is Notre Dame today is made up of the bits and pieces of their dedicated lives. Teachers, especially, affect eternity, never knowing, as Henry Adams noted, "where their influence stops." Generations of young men, and now young women, have been touched during a formative period of young adulthood by Notre Dame. The common metaphor is of family, a metaphor one is reminded of when graduates wander through the renovated Main Building and talk with pride of "our building."

To Notre Dame people, the past and present are of one weave... and thus this book.

Edward A. Malloy, ""

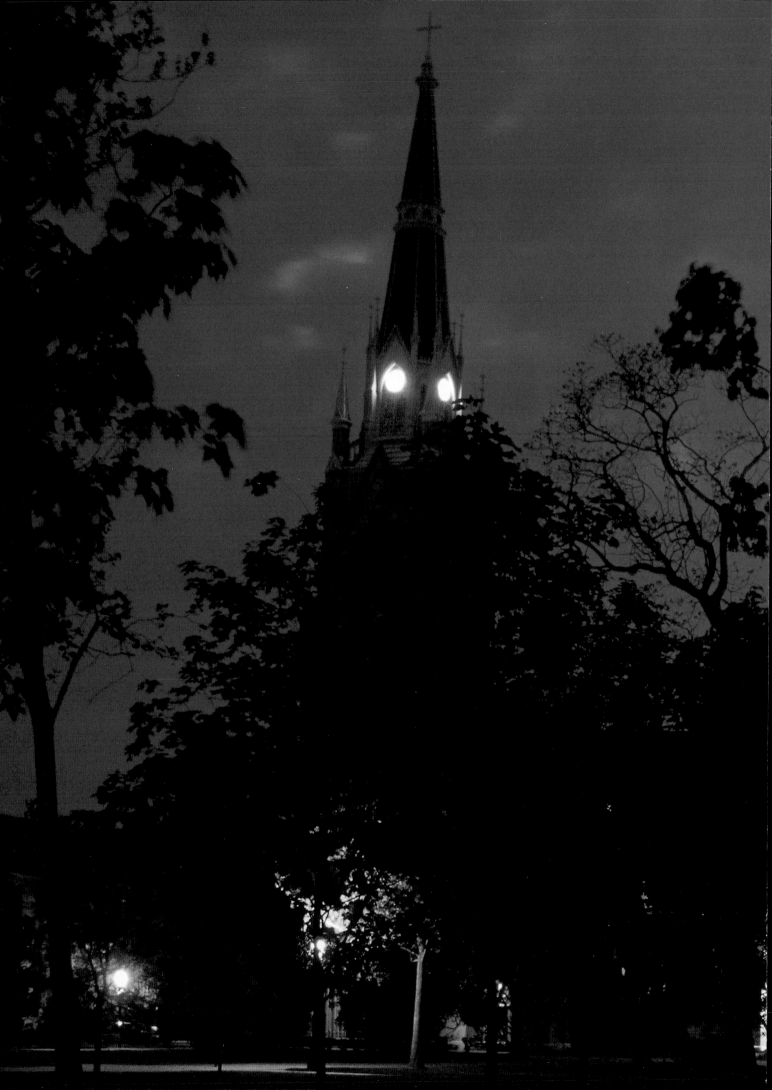

An outdoor class in the DeBartolo Quad pergola

Sometimes in mid–May or late September there comes a day suitable for framing. The campus is so lovely that you realize that God would enroll at Notre Dame, if he could afford it.

–Edward Fischer

I have seen, where a strange country
Opened its secret plains about me,
One great golden dome stand lonely with its golden image, one
Seen afar, in strange fulfillment,
Through the sunlit Indian summer

From a poem , "The Arena," by G.K. Chesterton after a visit to Notre Dame

The "Word of Life" mural, Hestburgh Library

Tom Dooley

Father Edward Sorin, CSC

I can use the word "soul" at Notre Dame and they don't snicker.

Norman Mailer

Grotto of Our Lady of Lourdes

DeBartolo Quadrangle

College of Business

DeBartolo Hall

College of Business

Bond Hall (School of Architecture)

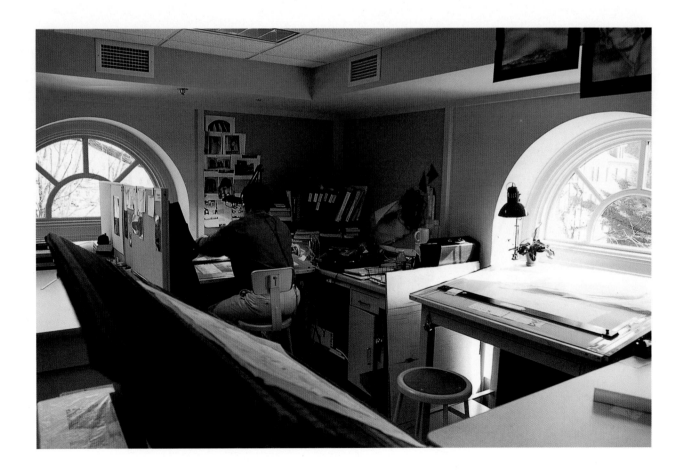

Keough (right) and McGlinn Residence Halls

Blessed Brother Andre, CSC

Eck Center (Alumni Association and Visitors' Center)

Hesburgh Center for International Studies

"Reckers" restaurant in expanded South Dining Hall

Clarke Memorial Fountain

Eck Center (Hammes-Notre Dame Bookstore), Father Anthony Lauck's "Visitation," foreground

*Education without religion or moral training is a very dangerous thing...It is time for the educators of the country
to take this matter into consideration. The sooner they do, the sooner we may look for a nation of citizens
whose lives will be an example of truth, honor, justice, and all that makes men noble.*

Rev. William Corby, C.S.C.

Basilica of the Sacred Heart

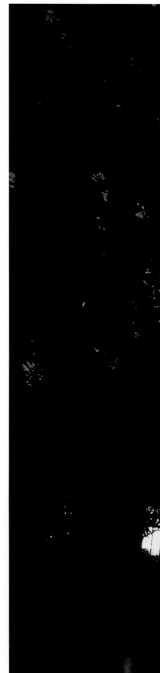

On a cool, sweet morning in early June there is nothing in the world more fresh than this campus.
On an October afternoon with the lakes reflecting bright colors and the dome shimmering in the
Indian summer sun, the whole world hums with contentment. When an August night is filled
with the whir of crickets and cicadas, it hints of autumn and of time running out.

Edward Fischer

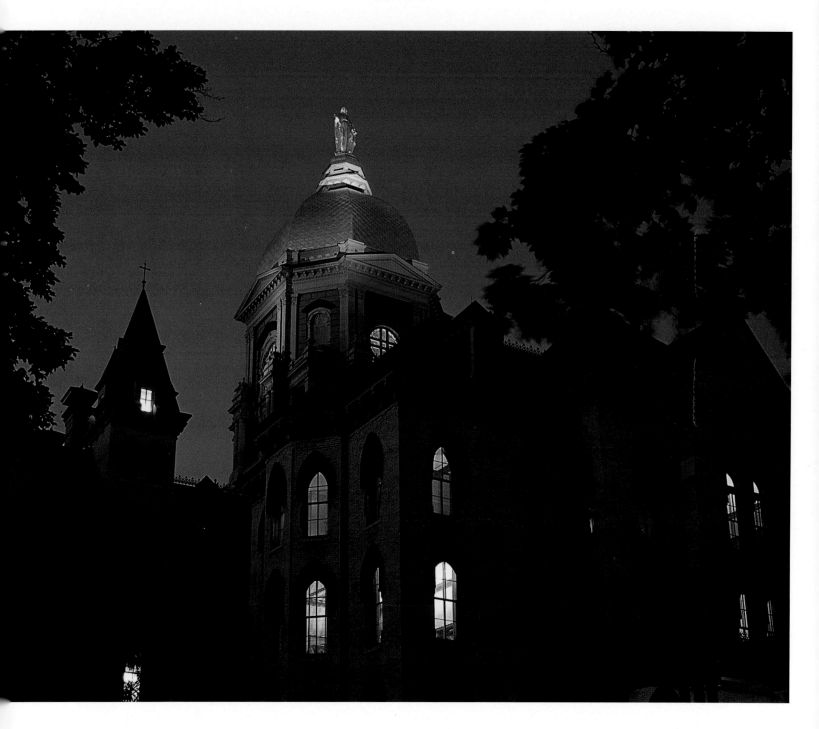

The Main Building reopened in July 1999, restored to its Victorian elegance

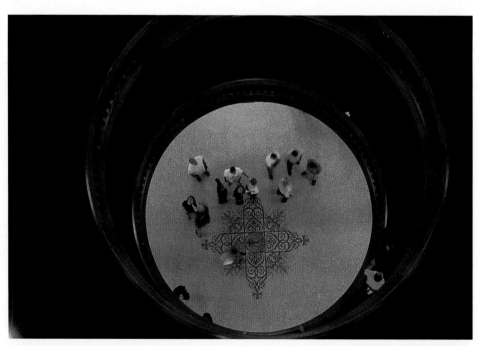

The Columbus murals

Admissions area

Reception area, President's Office

Classroom

Contemporary residence hall room, Pasquerilla West

Biological Sciences class in Juday Creek

Mass on the Feast of Our Lady of Guadalupe

Women's crew

Marian Kennedy Fischer Hall, London

Modernized locker room in expanded Notre Dame Stadium

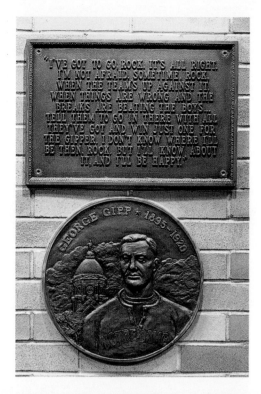

"I'VE GOT TO GO, ROCK. IT'S ALL RIGHT. I'M NOT AFRAID. SOMETIME, ROCK, WHEN THE TEAM'S UP AGAINST IT, WHEN THINGS ARE WRONG AND THE BREAKS ARE BEATING THE BOYS, TELL THEM TO GO IN THERE WITH ALL THEY'VE GOT AND WIN JUST ONE FOR THE GIPPER. I DON'T KNOW WHERE I'LL BE THEN, ROCK, BUT I'LL KNOW ABOUT IT, AND I'LL BE HAPPY."

GEORGE GIPP · 1895–1920

'Fighting Irish' began as a slur—term of opprobrium.
But we took it up and made of it a badge of honor,
a symbol of fidelity and courage to everyone who suffers
from discrimination, to everyone who has an uphill
fight for the elemental decencies and the basic Christian
principles woven into the texture of our nation.

Rev. Charles M. Carey, C.S.C.

For being Irish American and not wanting Notre Dame to win one for the Gipper is like being Native American and not wanting the Sioux to win one for Sitting Bull. It puts one in a culturally untenable position. It makes people suspicious of one's true background. And it ensures that one will spend all eternity in the deepest, dankest pit of hell.

Joe Queenan

*Generations of Notre Dame men have trod
the paths about and around the lakes.
Many a future has been planned on these
paths, many an urgent problem solved.*

1924–25 Undergraduate Manual

Student body and faculty posed in front of the Main Building, circa 1870.

A selection of vintage historical photographs from the Notre Dame Archives – Compiled by Charles Lamb and Marlene Wasikowski

FOOTFALLS THROUGH THE AGES

otre Dame is a "carried book." It is mythos and ethos, a long-descending blessing, a narrative written over generations, a tradition revered and reinterpreted by succeeding waves of young people. The insouciant youngster lounging in a nineteenth Century study hall becomes the occupant of a computer niche in the School of Architecture. Stiff Victorian poses fade into pergola classrooms. Bookstore basketball replaces marbles as recreation. Names scrawled in old brick give way to modern buildings. Religious iconography evolves from statuary to the compelling human embrace of Father Lauck's "Visitation." Thus is Notre Dame seen in time.

The Log Chapel as it stands on campus today. It is a reconstruction of the Chapel that was in use in the earliest days of the University.

1686

Father Claude Allowez founds the mission of Saint Mary of the Lakes on the shore of Saint Mary's Lake.

1832

Father Stephen Badin establishes his mission on the shore of Saint Mary's Lake, in the vicinity of the site of the present Log Chapel.

1838

The local Potawatomi Indians are forced from their land by the U.S. military. Father Petit accompanies the Indians on their forced journey to a reservation, but dies in Missouri at the age of 27. His remains are interred in the Log Chapel.

1842

Holy Cross priest Father Edward Sorin and several brothers of the community, eventually known as the Holy Cross Brothers, arrive at the site of Badin's mission to found the University of Notre Dame du Lac.

(November 30) Father Sorin says his first Mass in the original Log Chapel.

Alexis Coquillard and Clement Reckers become the University's first students.

Father Sorin begins a tradition of giving packages of food to local Potawatomi Indians at Christmas.

Father Edward Sorin, CSC, Notre Dame's founder and first president.

1843

Sorin creates the Manual Labor School for boys 12 to 21.

The first Holy Cross sisters arrive at Notre Dame.

The University's first building, now called Old College, is constructed.

1844

The University of Notre Dame is officially chartered by the State of Indiana.

1846

The Notre Dame Band is founded.

1847

Father Sorin begins selling bricks made on campus from the marl of Saint Mary's Lake. The price is $3 a thousand.

1848

Construction begins on the University's first Sacred Heart Church, which is completed in 1852.

The University's program is divided for the first time between the classical course and the commercial course.

1849

The first real "Commencement" is held with two graduates.

Notre Dame is a place, a sequence in time, and an immediate, living fact all wrapped round with people.

Richard Sullivan

Artist's rendition of the Notre Dame campus in the mid 1850s. The scene includes the first Main Building and the first Sacred Heart Church.

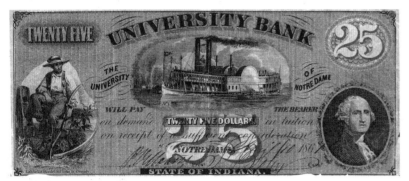

Script issued by Notre Dame during the Civil War.

1850

Father Sorin dispatches a group of Holy Cross brothers and laymen to California to take part in the Gold Rush.

1851

Notre Dame is granted its first Post Office, and Father Sorin is appointed postmaster.

1856

1850 1851 1856 The bell carillon is installed in the original Sacred Heart Church. Today it is part of the present Basilica of the Sacred Heart and is the oldest carillon in North America.

1861

The University creates the Department of Commerce.

1861–5

During the Civil War, the Notre Dame community sends seven priests to serve as chaplains and more than 80 Holy Cross sisters to serve as nurses for the Union Army.

1861–9

The University issues its own "money"–"University Bank" scrip in denominations of $1, $5, $10, $25, and $50.

1863

The first physics and geology courses are taught at Notre Dame.

1865

Construction begins on a second Main Building for the University. The plans include a dome topped by a statue of the Virgin Mary.

Father Sorin starts Ave Maria Press.

Rev. Patrick Dillon, C.S.C., succeeds Father Edward Sorin and becomes the University's second president.

The Notre Dame faculty consists of 34 professors.

The University creates the Department of Science and awards its first science degree.

1866

Rev. William Corby, C.S.C., becomes the University's third president.

The University's observatory is established with a gift of a telescope from Napoleon, III, Emperor of the French.

1867

The first issue of the Scholastic is published.

1869

The Notre Dame Law School, first Catholic law school in the United States, opens.

1868

The Notre Dame Alumni Association is formed.

Time marked its ceaseless course through the terrible burning, even as it had done in the hours of peace, study and prayer. We shall never forget that bell, unruffled and peaceful, as it was heard, and barely heard, amid the crackling and roaring of the flames, the falling of walls, the noise of the engine, the rushing and hissing of water and the loud shouts of men – the peaceful but appalling sound of these sweet church bells striking the hours of God's ever passing time, His quiet, all–embracing Eternity.

Scholastic, June 1879

View of the aftermath of the fire that destroyed the Main Building in 1879. The current Main Building was constructed following the fire.

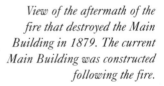

1870

Construction begins on the University's second Sacred Heart Church (now the Basilica of the Sacred Heart.) It is consecrated 1888.

1871

Students for the first time are permitted to go home for the Christmas holidays.

1872

Rev. Auguste Lemonnier, C.S.C., becomes the University's fourth president.

1873

Lemonnier conceives and establishes a circulating library believed to be the first in American Catholic higher education.

Notre Dame establishes the first Engineering School at a Catholic university.

The stained glass windows are installed in Sacred Heart Church.

Students and faculty on the steps of the newly constructed Main Building. This is believed to be the earliest photograph of the building, taken just as construction was completed in the fall of 1879.

1874

Father Lemonnier dies; Rev. Patrick Colovin, C.S.C., becomes the University's fifth president.

Luigi Gregori, court painter to Pope Pius IX, arrives at Notre Dame to become the University's artist–in–residence (until 1891).

1875

The first Eucharist is celebrated in Sacred Heart Church.

1877

Rev. William Corby, C.S.C., serves a second term as the University's president.

1879

(April) A fire destroys the University's Main Building, along with several other buildings. Shortly after the fire, work begins on the present Main Building. It is ready in time for fall classes.

Tuition, room, board and bedding, etc. is $125 per semester.

Crew of the "Evangeline" on St. Joseph Lake, 1888.

1880s

The Grounds Department, under Brother Philip Kunze, begins work on the arboretum in the University's main quadrangle.

1881

Washington Hall is constructed.

Rev. Thomas Walsh, C.S.C., becomes the University's sixth president.

1882

St. Edward's Hall is opened as the University's grade school (today it serves as a men's dormitory).

1883

Science Hall (now LaFortune Student Center) is constructed.

The first annual Laetare Medal is awarded.

1885

Notre Dame becomes the first American university to install electric lighting.

A class in the natural sciences (possibly zoology) posed with specimens from the University's Museum of Natural History, circa 1880.

1886

The Golden Dome is gilded for the first time.

Holy Cross Hall is constructed as a seminary. It will be converted to a men's dormitory in 1967 and razed in 1990.

1887

Notre Dame plays its first football game against another university (Michigan).

1888

James Burns, future Notre Dame president, is graduated from the University's Manual Labor School as a painter.

1888–9

Sorin Hall—Catholic education's first residence hall with private rooms– is constructed. Father Sorin himself blesses the cornerstone.

Notre Dame's volunteer firemen on the Main Quad, circa 1899.

1890

Luigi Gregori executes the 12 murals depicting the life of Christopher Columbus on the walls of the main hall of the Main Building.

1892

"Return of Columbus and Reception at Court," one of Gregori's Columbus murals, is used by the United States Post Office as the design for a stamp to commemorate the 400th anniversary of Columbus's first voyage.

1893

Father Sorin dies at the age of 79.

Notre Dame mathematician and aeronautical researcher, Dr. Albert Zahm, presents a paper titled "Stability of Aeroplanes and Flying Machines."

The Sacred Heart statue in front of the Main Building is dedicated.

The University sponsors its own exhibit at the Columbian Exposition in Chicago.

University President Walsh dies; Rev. Andrew Morrissey, C.S.C., becomes the University's seventh president.

Corby Hall is built as a residence for teaching priests.

Football ticket office at Cartier Field, 1894.

1896

Colonel John R. Fellows, District Attorney of New York City, establishes the first scholarship at Notre Dame.

Father John Zahm, a Notre Dame professor, writes that evolutionary theory and Catholicism are compatible.

The Grotto of Our Lady of Lourdes is dedicated.

1898

A sample menu from the University kitchen includes such items as oxtail soup, veal, dumplings, rutabaga, split peas and grape pie.

John Shillington, a former Notre Dame student, is killed in the explosion of the battleship Maine in Havana harbor. A memorial to Shillington stands outside Gate 8 of the Joyce Athletic and Convocation Center.

1899

The first wireless message transmitted in the U.S. is achieved by Jerome Green, a Notre Dame professor and researcher.

The discovery of something absolutely new is the object of research.
Not immediate usefulness, but new truth is the goal, and it is to be
sought for its own sake in the long term awareness that it may
turn out to be useful in the future, but with the pursuit geared to
the illusive thing rather than any quick, practical utility.

Richard Sullivan

An electrical engineering class at work in the early 1890s.

Room in Sorin Hall, 1893.

Interhall baseball team from Corby Hall, 1904.

1904

Notre Dame alumnus, Frank Hering, calls for a national holiday in honor of mothers. The idea later evolves into Mothers' Day.

William Butler Yeats visits Notre Dame.

1905

Rev. John W. Cavanaugh, C.S.C., becomes the University's eighth president.

1906

The statue of Father Sorin is unveiled on the main quadrangle.

"The Notre Dame Victory March" is composed by two brothers, Michael and John Shea, both students.

1908

The student population passes 1,000 for the first time.

Father Julius Nieuwland, discoverer of formulae that led to synthetic rubber, with students in his chemistry lab, circa 1915.

1909

Notre Dame scientist Rev. Julius Nieuwland, C.S.C., founds the magazine, the *American Midland Naturalist*.

A student strikes a relaxed pose in one of the study halls located in the Main Building, circa 1900.

*Military training
at Notre Dame,
circa 1915.*

1911

A statue of Father William Corby administrating absolution during the battle of Gettysburg is erected in front of Corby Hall; it replicates a statue on the battlefield in Pennsylvania.

1916

A mob of Notre Dame students burns a South Bend street car to protest the beating of two students by men allegedly employed for the purpose by the street car company.

1919

Eamon de Valera, first president of the Irish Free State, visits Notre Dame.

Rev. James Burns, C.S.C., becomes the University's ninth president.

The Manual Labor School is phased out.

The Notre Dame Glee Club aboard train on a concert tour, circa 1912.

The yearbook staff at work on the 1915 edition of The Dome.

*His daily drama was played out at noon on the porch of Sorin, where he sniffed letters
for hints of perfume, rolled his eyes heavenward, read aloud return addresses, made
comments, and sailed each envelope with true aim into the eye of the uneasy recipient.*

Edward Fischer describing Sorin Hall Rector, Rev. John (Pop) Farley, C.S.C.

Campus marble competition, 1913.

Campus bakers with loaves of the famous Notre Dame bread, circa 1912.

Brother Leo Donovan posing with one of the work horses on the Notre Dame Farms managed by the Brothers of Holy Cross, circa 1910. Six members of the religious community eventually known as the Brothers of Holy Cross accompanied Father Sorin when he arrived at the site of the University in 1842, and the brothers were an integral part of the University's development.

St. Edward's Hall and gardens, home to the minims (Notre Dame's grade school students), 1920.

1920

Notre Dame tuition is $170; room and board is $404.

Theology courses are included in the University's formal curriculum

University President Burns appoints a lay Board of Trustees to supervise fund-raising.

Rev. John O'Hara, C.S.C., future University president, founds The Religious Bulletin.

1922

Rev. Bernard Lange, C.S.C., a dedicated bodybuilder, is acclaimed the fourth–strongest man in the world.

Rev. Matthew Walsh, C.S.C., becomes the University's tenth president.

1923

Architect Frank Lloyd Wright visits Notre Dame; he apparently conceives a plan for the future development of the campus, but no copy of the plan survives.

Notre Dame students and local immigrant workers clash with the Ku Klux Klan in South Bend, resulting in the Klan being "run out of town."

Sorin Hall is equipped with indoor plumbing.

The World War I Memorial Entrance–incorporating the motto "God, Country, Notre Dame"–is added to Sacred Heart Church.

Notre Dame's youngest students prepare for their weekly bicycle outing. They are posed in front of a statue of St. Edward.

1924

The University creates a Faculty Board of Athletics to oversee the academic progress of student athletes.

University President Walsh refuses to allow fraternities at Notre Dame (even Phi Beta Kappa).

1925

Notre Dame and the Four Horsemen beat Stanford and Ernie Nevers in the only Rose Bowl appearance by the Irish.

1928

Rev. Charles O'Donnell, C.S.C., becomes the University's eleventh president.

1929

The Notre Dame grade school is closed.

Knute Rockne with unidentified players, 1920's.

Interhall football game, Walsh versus Badin, 1920.

FOOTBALL
Notre Dame vs Stanford

January 1st, 1925, 2:15 p. m.

ROSE BOWL

Price $5.00

Tax Exempt

SEC. C
ROW 16
SEAT 2
ENTER
TUNNEL 17
Notre Dame vs. Stanford
January 1, 1925, at 2:15 p. m.
ROSE BOWL, PASADENA
RETAIN THIS CHECK

Ticket to the 1925 Rose Bowl, the last game for the Four Horsemen.

The marching band on the steps of the Main Building, 1928

View out the front door of the Main Building, circa 1920.

Commencement on the Main Quad, 1932.

Franklin Delano Roosevelt receives an honorary degree from University President Father John O'Hara, CSC, in December of 1935. Roosevelt was the first sitting president to visit the Notre Dame campus.

1931

Father Julius Nieuwland,
a Notre Dame priest and
chemistry professor,
develops the formulae
for synthetic rubber.

Notre Dame football coach,
Knute Rockne, is killed in
a plane crash.

1932

Lay faculty members
outnumber religious
faculty 3 to 1.

The Graduate School
is officially established.

1934

Rev. John O'Hara, C.S.C.,
becomes the University's
twelfth president.

1935

Franklin Roosevelt becomes
the first U.S. president to visit
Notre Dame while in office.

1939

Professor Waldemar Gurian
begins publishing The
Review of Politics.

Naval training unit at Notre Dame during World War II.

1940

Rev. J. Hugh O'Donnell, C.S.C., becomes the University's thirteenth president.

The movie "Knute Rockne, All–American" is filmed on the campus and later is premiered in downtown South Bend.

1942–6

In this four–year period, 11,925 men complete officer's training at Notre Dame.

1942

The University of Notre Dame celebrates its Centennial; tuition is $330; room and board costs are $459.

1943

Martin J. Gillen bequeaths his 6,000–acre estate in far northern Wisconsin to be used as a boy's summer camp and a retreat for Holy Cross religious. The property ultimately will be the site of Notre Dame's Environmental Research Center.

Saturday inspection of Waves, who also trained on campus during World War II, circa 1945.

1946

Rev. John J. Cavanaugh, C.S.C., becomes the fourteenth president of the University.

The University purchases 39 prisoner–of–war barracks from the U.S. government to house the families of married veterans attending Notre Dame. This new campus housing is christened "Vetville."

A young Holy Cross priest named Hesburgh is made chaplain of "Vetville."

1947

Notre Dame's Medieval Institute is founded.

The Notre Dame Foundation is formed to serve as a fund–raising apparatus for the University. As a result, the University's first permanent endowment is established.

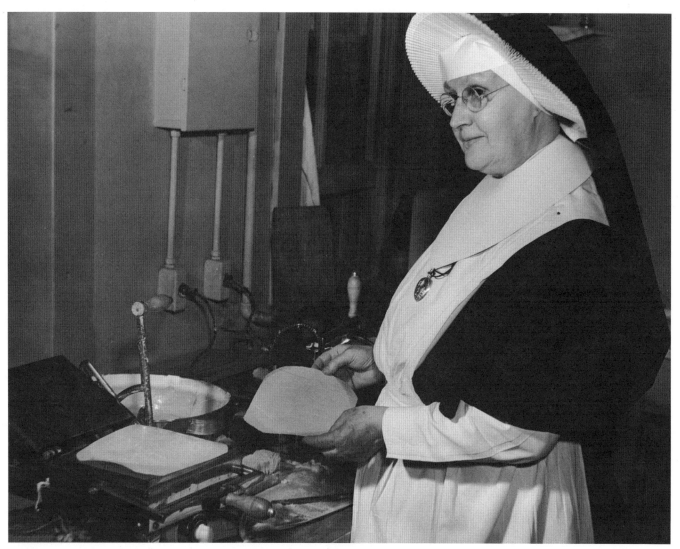

Sister Zigmunda of the Holy Cross Congregation making communion hosts, 1957. The Sisters of the Holy Cross were an important part of campus life, from teaching the minims to infrastructure tasks such as cooking, baking, laundering and tailoring. Photograph courtesy of the Sisters of the Holy Cross Congregational Archives.

1952

Rev. Theodore Hesburgh, C.S.C., becomes the University's fifteenth president.

1955

Ivan Mestrovic's masterpiece, Descent from the Cross, is installed in Sacred Heart Church.

1958

Father Hesburgh becomes a member of the U.S. Civil Rights Commission.

Moreau Seminary is completed on the shore of Saint Joseph's Lake.

The convent of the Holy Cross Sisters closes, ending an era of service by the sisters to the Notre Dame campus. They are destined for a new role in the University with the coming of coeducation in 1972.

If you want to belong, you have to learn the myth. You have to wrap your heart and mind in it. You have to believe the meanest rocks of the place tell a story...Behind the myths is a cast of hundreds, working in loyalty for the Notre Dame of their dreams, in a love affair that lasts a lifetime.

Rev. Robert Griffin, C.S.C.

Vetville scene, 1950s.

Summer student in chemistry lab, 1950. Women religious pursued graduate degrees at Notre Dame before the advent of undergraduate coeducation.

Stations of the Cross, circa 1950

The legendary professor of English Frank O'Malley in the classroom, 1950s. His most remembered quote, "Their blood is in the bricks," aptly described the bachelor dons of Notre Dame, as well as others who gave their lives to the University.

Morrissey Hall, circa 1950.

Students decorate campus in anticipation of the USC game, 1960s.

1960

Notre Dame is one of six universities to receive a $6 million grant from the Ford Foundation as "a center of academic excellence."

1961-3

The Memorial Library (now the Theodore M. Hesburgh Library) is constructed.

1963

Notre Dame's Radiation Research Building is completed. Funded by the U. S. Department of Energy, the Rad Lab annually attracts the world's largest university concentration of radiation chemists.

Father Theodore Hesburgh with student leaders, including Student Body President David Krashna (at the far right), 1970.

1964

The famous *The Word of Life* mosaic is installed on the south facade of the Memorial Library. It is composed of 5,714 individual pieces.

1965

Sister Suzanne Kelly, O.S.B., and Josephine Massyngbaerde Ford become the University's first tenured women faculty members.

1967

Governance of Notre Dame is transferred from the Congregation of Holy Cross to a Board of Trustees composed predominantly of lay women and men.

1969

Father Hesburgh issues his "15–minute" rule for student demonstrators–if they refuse to cease and desist after that time, they will face arrest or expulsion.

Students protest recruitment visits to campus by the Dow Chemical Company and the CIA, 1968.

Robert Kennedy visits Notre Dame during the presidential primaries, April 1968.

Unidentified long jumper competing in the Notre Dame Fieldhouse, 1960s.

The arrival of coeducation at Notre Dame was celebrated with a picnic in the fall of 1972.

1970

The Burke Memorial Golf Course abandons a 40–year tradition by allowing women to play on the course.

1972

The first women under–graduates are enrolled at Notre Dame.

President Richard Nixon removes Father Hesburgh from the chairmanship of the Civil Rights Commission after Hesburgh criticizes Nixon's civil rights record.

1974

Francis J. "Frank" O'Malley, Notre Dame professor and campus institution, dies.

Notre Dame has its first woman valedictorian.

Bengal bout match, 1977.

Protests held on campus following the invasion of Cambodia and the killings at Kent State, May 1970.

*I remember the late–night sound of someone bouncing a basketball on
the court behind Walsh; the late–night smell of doughnuts baking in
North Dining Hall; my freshman roommate waking me up early
one morning to share the excitement of her first snow.*

Sally Stanton MacKenzie

Bookstore basketball game, 1977.

Left: Art studios in the old Fieldhouse, 1970s.

Right: Father Theodore Hesburgh celebrating his 25 anniversary as University president, 1978.

Mass in Sacred Heart Basilica celebrated by University Chaplain Father William Toohey, CSC, 1976.

Professor Emil T. Hofman administering a final chemistry exam, December 1983. He taught an estimated 30,000 students in his tenure.

1980

The Snite Museum of Art is completed.

1982

Father Hesburgh enters the Guinness Book of World Records as the person with the most honorary college degrees.

1986

The Clarke Memorial Fountain is dedicated in memory of members of the Notre Dame community who died in World War II, the Korean War and the Vietnam War.

1988

President Ronald Reagan is guest of honor at the dedication ceremonies for the Knute Rockne postage stamp.

1987

Rev. Edward Malloy, C.S.C., becomes the University's sixteenth president.

Fathers Hesburgh and Joyce on motor scooters, given them upon their retirement in 1987.

University President Father Edward Malloy, CSC and President Ronald Reagan at a campus ceremony for the unveiling of a U.S. postage stamp honoring Knute Rockne, 1988.

View of the interior of Sacred Heart Basilica during renovation, 1989-1990.

1990

Sacred Heart Church is reopened after extensive renovations.

Sister Thea Bowman becomes the first African–American to be awarded the Laetare Medal.

1991

The Hesburgh Center for International Studies is dedicated. Mrs. Joan Kroc, widow of the McDonald's restaurant chain founder, underwrote its construction.

The postal service issues a postcard picturing the Main Building and commemorating the University's Sesquicentennial.

Father Malloy is elected to a second five–year term as president by the Board of Trustees.

The National Broadcasting Company contracts to telecast all Notre Dame home football games for five–year period, and the University commits income to student aid.

The Notre Dame Award is established to honor humanitarian service. Complementary to the Laetare Medal for American Catholics, it is interfaith and international.

CSC Priests gathered around University President Edward Malloy (in chair) on the steps of the newly renovated Main Building, 1999.

1992

De Bartolo Hall, a pioneering meld of computer and audio-visual educational technology, is dedicated.

1993

The feature film "Rudy," based on the story of a Notre Dame student who perseveres in his dream to play football, is released by Tri–Star Studios as the first movie allowed to film on campus since "Knute Rockne: All–American" in 1940.

1995

The new home of the College of Business Administration is dedicated.

1994

The School of Architecture is separated from the College of Engineering and made an autonomous academic unit.

View of Reckers, a cafe that was added to South Dining Hall in 1998.

1996

Notre Dame's endowment passes the $1 billion mark for the first time, ending the fiscal year at $1.227 billion.

1997

The $767–million "Generations: A Campaign for the Notre Dame Student" is launched as the most ambitious fund–raising initiative ever for a Catholic institution.

The expansion and renovation of Notre Dame Stadium is completed.

1998

The Keough–Notre Dame Study Centre, Ireland, is dedicated in a leased portion of historic Newman House in Dublin.

Main Building graffiti featuring two generations of Notre Dame students.

1999

2000

Marion Kennedy Fischer Hall, the University's new headquarters for educational programs in London, opens in the southeast corner of Trafalgar Square and is dedicated during the first international meeting of the Notre Dame Board of Trustees.

The Eck Center complex, containing a new Hammes Bookstore, as well as a Visitors' Center and Alumni Association offices, is opened on campus.

The Main Building is reopened after a two–year renovation.

The Institute for Latino Studies is established at Notre Dame.

December 1999

Alma Mater

Notre Dame, Our Mother, tender, strong and true

Proudly in the heavens gleams thy gold and blue.

Glory's mantle cloaks thee, golden is thy fame

And our hearts forever praise thee, Notre Dame:

And our hearts forever love thee, Notre Dame.

Community... At Notre Dame, the experience of students and faculty encompasses the scope of humanity. Represented on the campus are students from all 50 states and 100 foreign countries, making Notre Dame this country's *most* national university.

Academics... Long ranked among America's Top 20 national research universities (U.S. News & World Report), Notre Dame is home to a variety of individual programs, institutes, and centers of excellence considered among the finest anywhere in the world.

Residence Life... About 80 percent of Notre Dame's roughly 8,000 undergraduates reside on campus, sharing in the daily triumphs and sometimes tragedies of life, and continuing one of the university's founding principals: that community fosters learning.

Catholic Character... Unlike many U.S. colleges and universities that have moved away from their church-based origins, Notre Dame continues to embrace its religious heritage. 'Catholic' means universal, and at Notre Dame that translates not only into vigorous scientific and scholarly examination of all of Creation, but also into sharing God's blessings through service to others.

Father Sorin [above, with Notre Dame faculty, circa 1880] described the first events in Notre Dame's history to his religious superior, Fr. Basil Moreau, in a remarkably prescient letter now replicated on a plaque [left] overlooking St. Mary's Lake and close to Old College [far left], the longest continuously existing building on the campus.

Three structures have served at one time or another as the university's Main Building, the most recent having welcomed visitors across its 'Salve' (Good day) threshold since 1879, while the bells - crafted in Le Mans, France - calling the faithful to prayer in the Basilica of the Sacred Heart comprise the oldest bell carillon in North America.

What is today a great international university began as a small Catholic outpost in the hinterlands of mid-19th century America. In fact, when the young French priest Fr. Edward Sorin and his band of six religious brothers of the Congregation of Holy Cross arrived at the eastern edge of St. Mary's Lake in 1842, they had but $300 and three dilapidated cabins with which to establish a school.

The cross atop the Basilica of the Sacred Heart stands as the highest man-made point on the Notre Dame campus, symbolizing the central place of faith in the life of the University. Constructed between 1869 and 1892, the basilica was so designated in 1992 by Pope John Paul II for its significance as a center of worship. A renovation that was completed in 1990 included restoration of the murals, gold leaf, and stained glass windows. Made by Carmelite nuns in the 19th century, the windows are among the few remaining examples of such design, most of those once found in Europe having been destroyed in World War II.

Notre Dame's founder, Rev. Edward Sorin, C.S.C., long sought to build a grotto on campus similar to the famed shrine in Lourdes, France. In 1896, three years after Sorin's death, the Grotto of Our Lady of Lourdes was constructed behind the basilica. A quiet spot to pray, reflect or light a candle, the grotto is one-seventh the size of its French inspiration.

Lourdes [above] is documented as being the oldest and largest example of its species in all of the surrounding county (and may actually pre-date the university's founding). More constant observers of the passing years include the sundial high on the east face of Dillon Hall and the four etched caricatures in the stone of Lyons Hall arch, a landmark beloved of untold thousands of Notre Dame men and women who have entered South Quad from under its graceful reach. Meanwhile, the memorial door on the east side of the Basilica of the Sacred Heart gives testimony to the enduring spirit of this special place.

God Country Notre Dame

IN GLORY EVERLASTING

Nearly ten generations of students have walked the Notre Dame campus, widely hailed as one of the most beautiful college environments in the country. The succession of Notre Dame fathers and sons, mothers and daughters has been marked in many ways. First by the seasonally alternating wardrobes of the more than 350 varieties of trees and shrubbery planted across the university's 800 central acres of land. The great sycamore tree located near the Grotto of Our Lady of

A s it holds for its faculty that excellence in research and
excellence in teaching *can* coexist, and even flourish, so
Notre Dame believes for its students that their academic
performance in the laboratory or classroom should not have to
be compromised by achievement on the athletic playing field.
Notre Dame rates among the top three American universities in
the graduation rate of *all* students and ranks second all-time in
the selection of Academic All-Americans. With a record 11
national championships (four of them won by legendary Coach
Frank Leahy [above]) and seven Heisman Trophy winners, no
college football program attracts more national attention or
contributes more to the academic mission of its university than

that of the Fighting Irish. In the past
decade, revenue from television broadcast
rights and bowl game appearances by the
Irish has provided tens of millions of
dollars for academic scholarships and
general financial assistance awarded to
nearly three-quarters of Notre Dame's
student body, athlete and non-athlete
alike. Since Notre Dame's last national
championship in football in 1988, several
women's athletic programs have emerged
into national prominence, resulting in
NCAA championships in women's
basketball, most recently, as well as in
women's soccer.

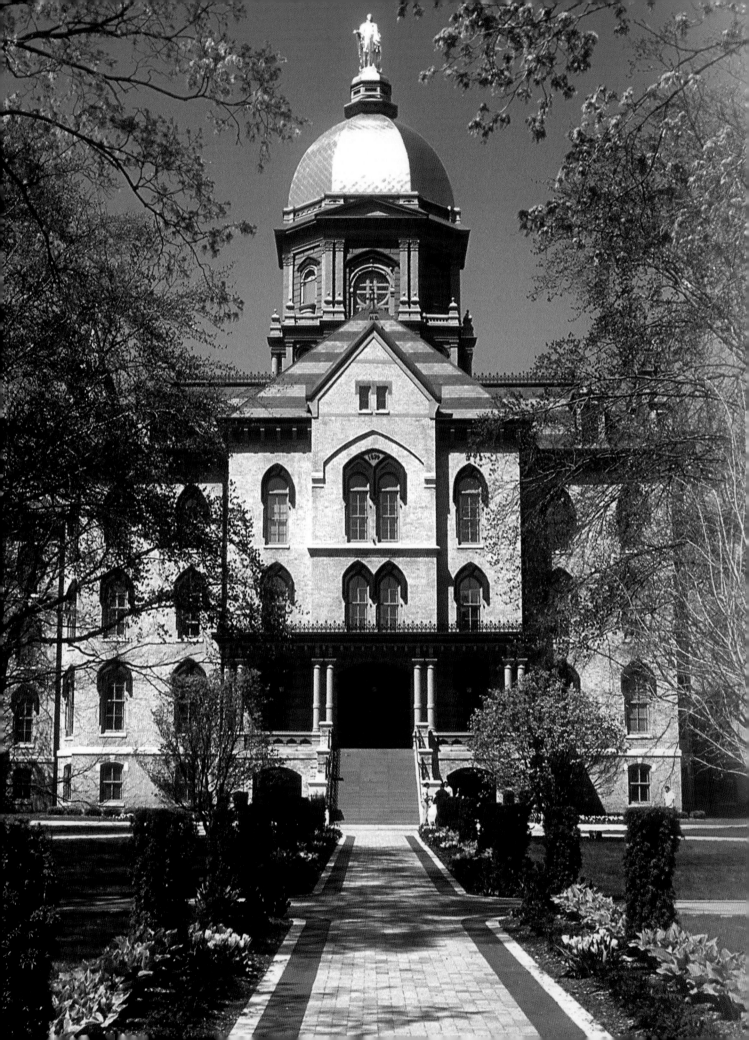

No college landmark in the world is better known than the Golden Dome of Notre Dame. So central is it to the University's identity that students and graduates are commonly called "Domers." The Main Building, upon which the dome stands, was constructed in 1879 after a massive fire destroyed the previous building on the site. A $58-million renovation of the Main Building, completed in 1999, restored its public areas to their Victorian-era elegance. The interior of the dome features 19th-century Vatican artist Luigi Gregori's allegorical representations of religion, philosophy, history, science, music, and poetry.

One of the world's most beautiful college campuses, Notre Dame exhibits four distinct faces. Winter - peacefully still under a virgin-white blanket of snow - paints a picture of what Father Sorin found on the plains of northern Indiana in November of 1842. The other seasons bring equal splendor. Spring - faithfully abloom in nature's new life. Summer - wonderfully lush under a canopy of green. Autumn - colorfully vivid in a blaze of red, orange, and yellow.

Where else is a college campus the Number 1 visitors attraction in its host state? The answer is: nowhere else but Notre Dame. Throughout the year the University welcomes upwards of half a million people; some for athletic contests, others for cultural and community events, and still more who just want to see the sights associated with one of the world's leading universities. The starting point for most is the Eck Visitor's Center [bottom right],

located along Notre Dame Avenue just south of the University's Main Circle. Opened in 1999 with the specific purpose of providing a place for the University to greet its many returning alumni and new visitors, the Eck Center is the launching point for organized walking tours of the campus, which - holding to another long Notre Dame tradition - are led by current students at the University. Though conducted regularly, tour schedules do vary according to whether classes are in session or not. So, if planning to take a guided campus tour, it may be best to check ahead.

Seven U.S. presidents have visited the Notre Dame campus, five of them to give the annual graduation address. The most recent was President George W. Bush, who not only followed his father into the Oval Office, but also onto the university's commencement stage, the senior President Bush speaking to the class of 1992. During the course of each academic year, the university also invites other prominent individuals from government and politics, important social organizations, the Church, the media, and the arts to speak to students and the broader community. Individuals like NBC Washington Bureau Chief and moderator of 'Meet the Press,' Tim Russert [top]. Other popular diversions on campus, meanwhile, include the annual Notre Dame Collegiate Jazz Festival [top right], the oldest college jazz festival in the nation. Also, 'Summer Shakespeare' in historic Washington Hall and the occasional popular music concert in the Joyce Convocation Center. Although the campus also provides opportunities to those looking for something a little more quiet and reflective - like the university's Snite Museum of Art, renowned for its world-class collection of pre-Columbian Meso-American art and artifacts.

While attaining excellence in teaching and scholarship, Notre Dame seeks to instill in its students a "sense of human solidarity and concern for the common good that will bear fruit as learning becomes service to justice." Notre Dame students learn to live in the residence halls, where 80 percent reside for all four years, and at the Coleman Family Center for Campus Ministry [far left], where

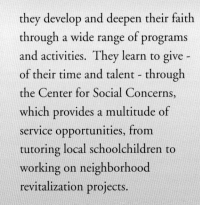

they develop and deepen their faith through a wide range of programs and activities. They learn to give - of their time and talent - through the Center for Social Concerns, which provides a multitude of service opportunities, from tutoring local schoolchildren to working on neighborhood revitalization projects.

Notre Dame...

Knowledge
TRADITION
Family
Faith

A closely knit community dedicated to
the life of the mind,
  • to scholarship and service
  • to values and vision
  • to soul and spirit
  • to hope and heritage

This is **NOTRE DAME**

the Faces of
Notre Dame

Photography by Kevin Burke, Heather K. Gollatz, and L. K. Dunn.
Additional photographs by Bill Steinmentz and William Strode.
Text by Dennis Brown, Notre Dame Department of Public Relations and Information.
Design by Perry Cooper and Kevin Burke. Printed by CFW Creative, Inc.
© University of Notre Dame, 2001